MONSTERGAMI

PAPER FOLDING FOR YOUR INNER MONSTER

MONSTERGAMI

PAPER FOLDING FOR YOUR INNER MONSTER

DUY NGUYEN

STERLING CHILDREN'S BOOKS
New York

STERLING CHILDREN'S BOOKS
New York

An Imprint of Sterling Publishing Co., Inc.
1166 Avenue of the Americas
New York, NY 10036

© 2015 by Duy Nguyen

ISBN 978-1-4549-1439-6

Distributed in Canada by Sterling Publishing Co., Inc.
c/o Canadian Manda Group, 664 Annette Street
Toronto, Ontario, Canada M6S 2C8
Distributed in the United Kingdom by GMC Distribution Services
Castle Place, 166 High Street, Lewes, East Sussex, England BN7 1XU
Distributed in Australia by NewSouth Books
45 Beach Street, Coogee, NSW 2034, Australia

For information about custom editions, special sales, and premium and corporate purchases,
please contact Sterling Special Sales at 800-805-5489 or specialsales@sterlingpublishing.com.

Manufactured in China

Lot #:
2 4 6 8 10 9 7 5 3
05/17

www.sterlingpublishing.com

Cover design by David Ter-Avanesyan
Back cover image © losw/Shutterstock

CONTENTS

INTRODUCTION 7

BASIC FOLDS AND SYMBOLS 8

    Legend 8

    Valley Fold 8

    Mountain Fold 8

    Kite Fold 8

    Inside Reverse Fold 9

    Outside Reverse Fold 9

    Pleat Fold 10

    Pleat Fold Reversed 10

    Squash Fold 1 10

    Squash Fold 2 11

    Inside Crimp Fold 11

    Outside Crimp Fold 11

BASE FOLDS 12

    Base Fold 1 12

    Base Fold 2 13

    Sink Fold 13

    Base Fold 3 14

    Base Fold 4 15

    Base Fold 5 16

MONSTERGAMI PROJECTS 17

    Headless Horseman 17

    Mummy 30

    Scarecrow 38

    Witch 50

    Wolf Man 58

    Zombie 66

    Frankenstein's Monster 74

    Creatue from the Black Lagoon 81

    Demon 88

    Three-Headed Dragon 96

    Dracula 103

    Alien 112

    Werewolf 117

INDEX 123

INTRODUCTION

It's a graveyard smash! Put these spooky origami projects together to cause mayhem. *Monstergami: Paper Folding for Your Inner Monster* will teach you the refined art of origami paper folding. It will also teach you how to disgust your friends and family with gross, scary MONSTERS! Disclaimer: if you were looking to make peace cranes, ponies, or puppies, you're in the wrong book. These frightening beasts would eat those cupcakes for breakfast! Instead, you'll find easy, step-by-step directions on how to transform regular paper into 13 heart-stopping monster origami projects sure to be a scream.

Monstergami includes 50 sheets of origami paper to construct an army of the undead. Create your own horror movie. Remember, once you've folded all the creatures, the fun is just beginning. Customize your monsters as much as you can stomach with markers, colored pencils, or stickers. The more gruesome, the better!

WARNING:

Fold at your own risk. Possible side-effects of *Monstergami* include a thirst for blood, uncontrollable urges to howl at the moon, and a hunger for human brains.

PAPER TIPS

The best origami paper is very thin, will keep a crease well, and fold flat. You can use plain white paper, color paper, or wrapping paper. Regular printer paper may be too heavy to make the many tight folds needed. Origami paper is available from craft and hobby shops. Unless otherwise indicated, the paper used to make these monsters is 6x6 inches. If you are having trouble, it may be easier to start out with larger paper.

GLUE TIPS

Use an easy-flowing paper glue. Use it sparingly; do not soak the paper. A toothpick makes a good applicator. After finishing a project, use glue as needed to prevent unfolding. After you've made your origami monster, give it time to dry. Avoid using glue sticks.

TECHNIQUE TIPS

Fold with care. Position the paper, especially at corners, precisely and see that edges line up before creasing a fold. Then use a fingernail to make a clean, flat crease. As you make folds, look to the next diagram for guidance. As you become more familiar with the folds, origami becomes easier and easier to accomplish. Try practicing the basic folds on seperate paper before starting the projects. This will make understanding the directions much easier.

BASIC FOLDS AND SYMBOLS

LEGEND

- - -	Valley Fold	- - - -	Inside Reverse Fold	→	Pleat Fold
- · - ·	Mountain Fold	◆	Scale	←	Fold Direction
++++++++	Cut	- - - -	Sink Fold	⌒→	Pull Direction
⟲→	Turn Over or Rotate	↔	Fold and Unfold	✳	For an extra challenge, complete this step or skip ahead

VALLEY FOLD

2. Completed VALLEY FOLD.

1. Fold forward.

MOUNTAIN FOLD

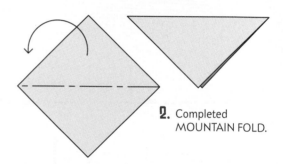

2. Completed MOUNTAIN FOLD.

1. Fold behind.

KITE FOLD

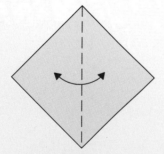

1. Valley fold and unfold making a center crease.

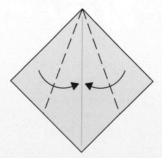

2. Valley folds. Fold both sides to the center crease.

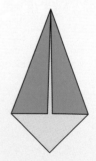

3. Completed KITE FOLD.

INSIDE REVERSE FOLD

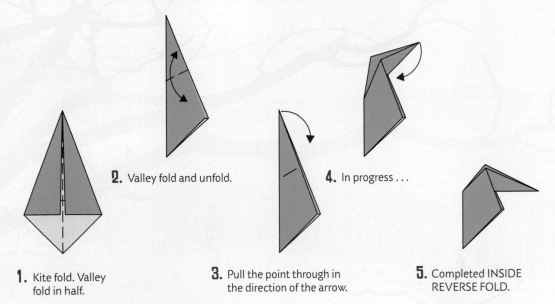

1. Kite fold. Valley fold in half.

2. Valley fold and unfold.

3. Pull the point through in the direction of the arrow.

4. In progress . . .

5. Completed INSIDE REVERSE FOLD.

OUTSIDE REVERSE FOLD

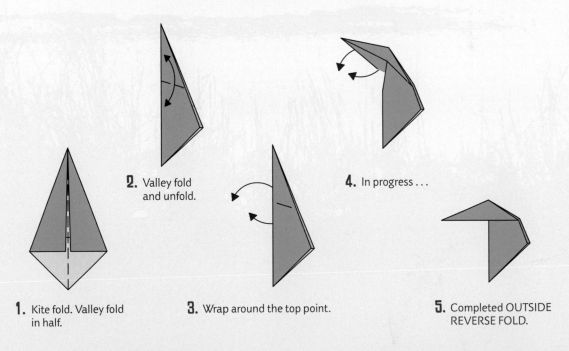

1. Kite fold. Valley fold in half.

2. Valley fold and unfold.

3. Wrap around the top point.

4. In progress . . .

5. Completed OUTSIDE REVERSE FOLD.

PLEAT FOLD

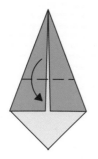

1. Kite fold. Valley fold.

2. Valley fold.

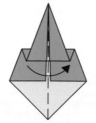

3. Fold in half.

4. Completed PLEAT FOLD.

PLEAT FOLD REVERSED

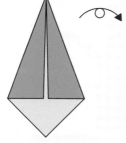

1. Kite fold. Turn over.

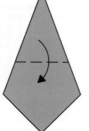

2. Valley fold.

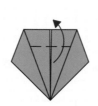

3. Valley fold.

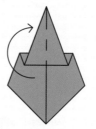

4. Mountain Fold.

5. Completed PLEAT FOLD REVERSED.

SQUASH FOLD 1

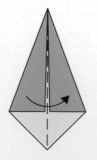

1. Kite fold. Valley fold.

2. Inside reverse fold.

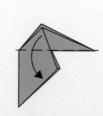

3. Valley fold.

4. Completed SQUASH FOLD 1.

SQUASH FOLD 2

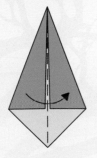 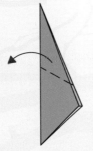  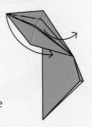 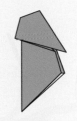

1. Kite fold.
Valley fold.

2. Valley fold.

3. Pull and fold. Open in the direction of the arrow.

4. Appearance before complete.

5. Completed SQUASH FOLD 2.

INSIDE CRIMP FOLD

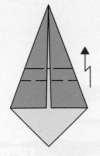 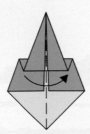 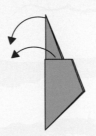 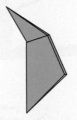

1. Kite fold.
Pleat fold.

2. Valley fold.

3. Pull and fold.

4. Completed INSIDE CRIMP FOLD.

OUTSIDE CRIMP FOLD

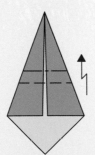 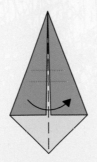  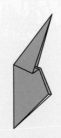

1. Pleat fold and unfold.

2. Valley fold.

3. Pull the flap down, allowing the sides to buckle at the joint.

4. Completed OUTSIDE CRIMP FOLD.

BASE FOLDS

BASE FOLD 1

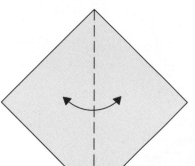

1. Valley fold and unfold.

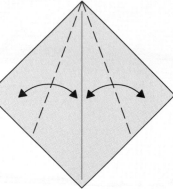

2. Valley fold both sides to the center crease, then unfold.

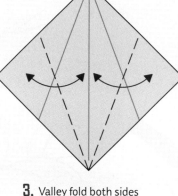

3. Valley fold both sides to the center crease, then unfold. Rotate.

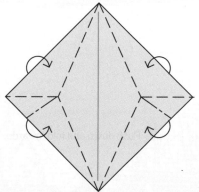

4. Pinch corners together and fold inward.

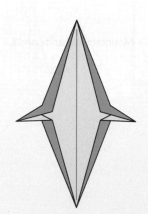

5. Appearance before complete.

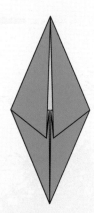

6. Completed BASE FOLD 1.

BASE FOLD 2

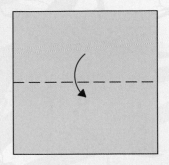

1. Valley fold.

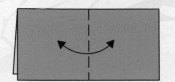

2. Valley fold and unfold.

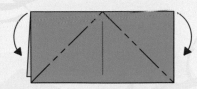

3. Inside reverse folds.

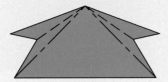

4. Appearance before complete.

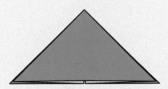

5. Completed BASE FOLD 2.

SINK FOLD

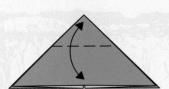

1. Base Fold 2. Valley fold and unfold.

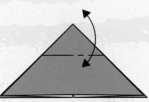

2. Mountain fold and unfold.

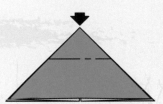

3. Push down and fold inward.

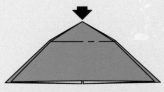

4. Appearance before complete.

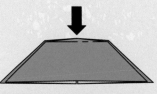

5. Appearance before complete.

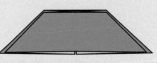

6. Completed SINK FOLD.

BASE FOLD 3

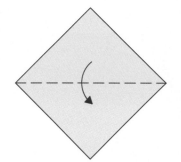

1. Valley fold.

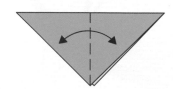

2. Valley fold and unfold.

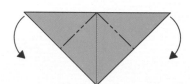

3. Inside reverse folds.

4. Valley fold and unfold.

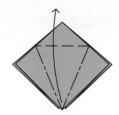

5. Pull top layer in direction of arrow and fold.

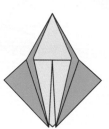

6. Before complete.

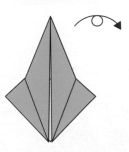

7. Turn over.

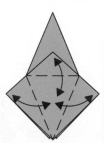

8. Valley fold and unfold.

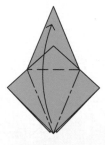

9. Pull top layer in direction. of arrow and fold.

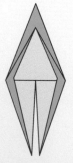

10. Appearance before complete.

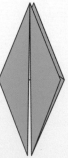

11. Completed BASE FOLD 3.

BASE FOLD 4

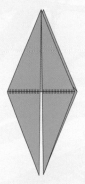 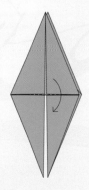  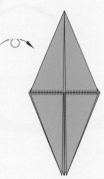

1. Base Fold 3. Cut the front layers.

2. Valley fold.

3. Turn over.

4. Cut the front layers.

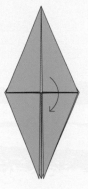 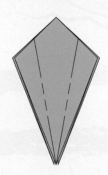

5. Valley fold.

6. Inside reverse folds.

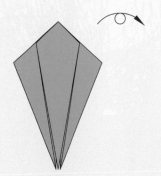 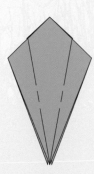 

7. Turn over.

8. Inside reverse folds.

9. Completed Base Fold 4.

BASE FOLD 5

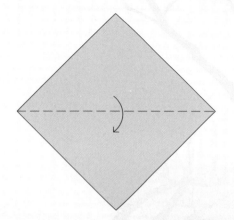

1. Valley fold diagonally in half.

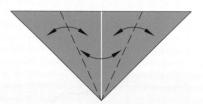

2. Valley fold and unfold.

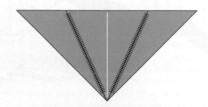

3. Cut as shown.

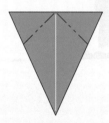

4. Inside reverse folds.

5. Open flaps.

6. Valley fold and unfold.

7. Squash folds.

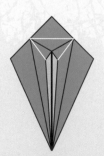

8. Before complete.

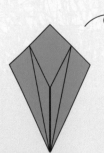

9. Turn over.

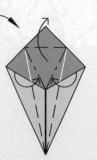

10. Repeat steps 6 and 7.

11. Open flaps.

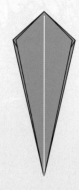

11. Completed BASE FOLD 5.

HEADLESS HORSEMAN

Sleepy Hollow? More like Creepy Hollow.
If you see this guy coming, try not to lose your head.

PART 1

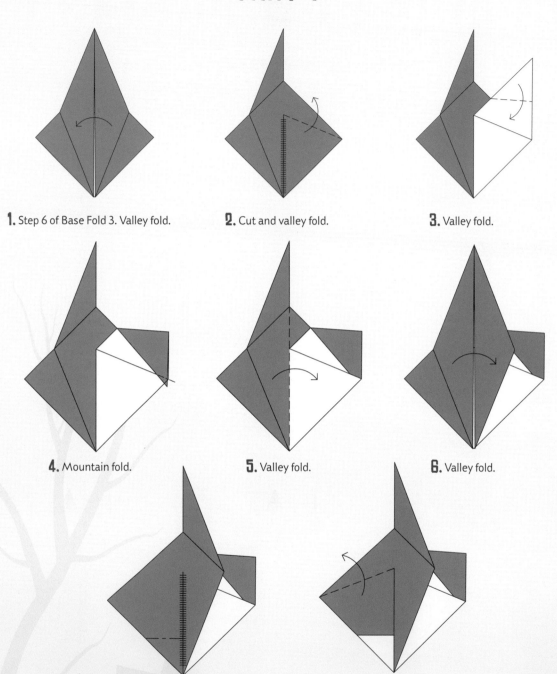

1. Step 6 of Base Fold 3. Valley fold.

2. Cut and valley fold.

3. Valley fold.

4. Mountain fold.

5. Valley fold.

6. Valley fold.

7. Cut and mountain fold.

8. Valley fold.

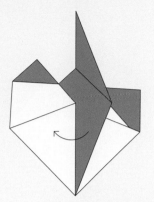

9. Valley fold.

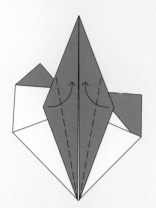

10. Valley folds.

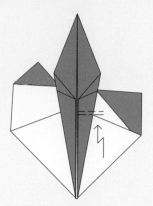

11. Crimp fold.

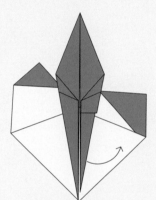

12. Pull and fold.

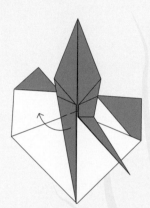

13. Outside reverse fold.

14. Inside reverse fold.

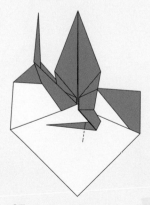

15. Inside reverse fold.

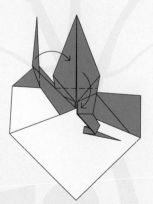

16. Valley folds.

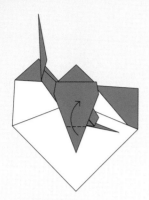

17. Valley fold.

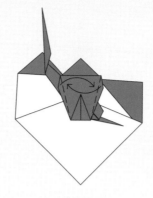

18. Valley folds.

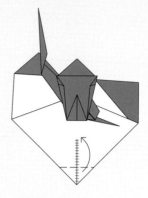

19. Cut and valley fold.

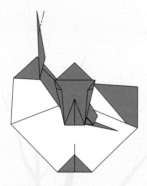

20. Inside reverse fold.

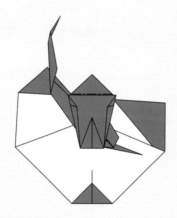

21. Mountain fold.

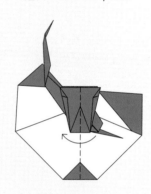

22. Valley fold.

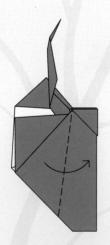

23. Valley fold.

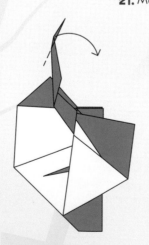

24. Valley fold.

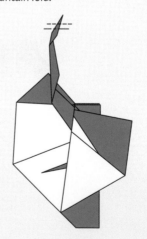

25. Pleat fold.

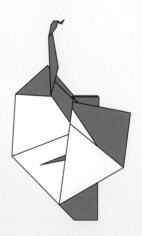

26. Completed PART 1.

PART 2

1. Base Fold 4.
Valley fold.

2. Inside reverse fold.

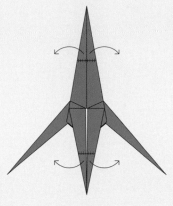

3. Cut the front and
valley fold.

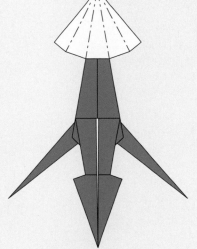

4. Mountain folds.

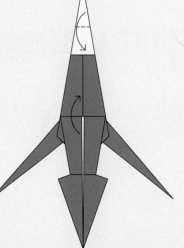

5. Valley folds.

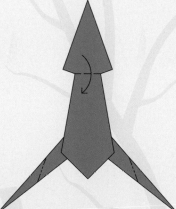

6. Valley fold and inside reverse folds.

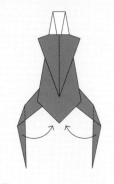

7. Valley fold both sides.

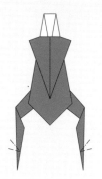

8. Crimp folds.

9. Valley fold in half.

10. Inside reverse fold.

11. Completed PART 2.

FIRST ASSEMBLY

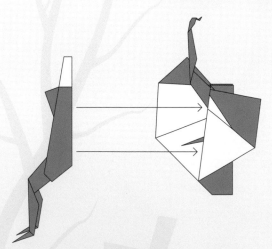

1. Join both parts together as indicated and apply glue to hold.

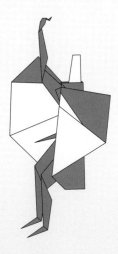

2. Completed FIRST ASSEMBLY.

PART 3

Cut origami paper into a 3.5- by 3.5-inch square.

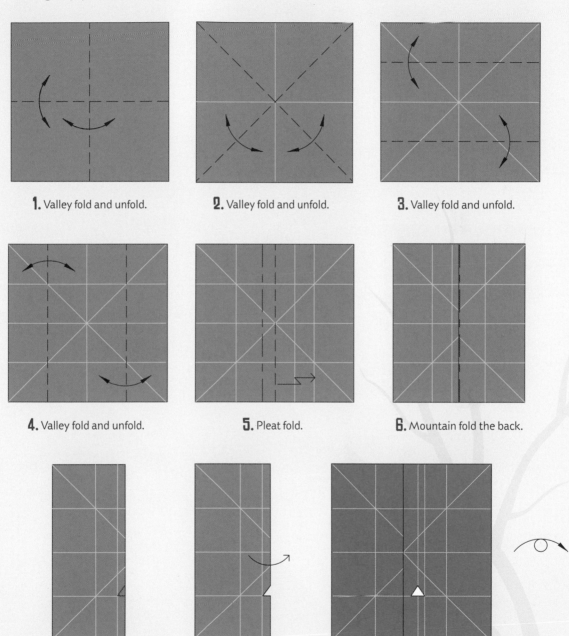

1. Valley fold and unfold.

2. Valley fold and unfold.

3. Valley fold and unfold.

4. Valley fold and unfold.

5. Pleat fold.

6. Mountain fold the back.

7. Cut as shown.

8. Valley fold to open out.

9. Turn over.

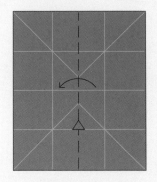

10. Valley fold.

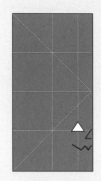

11. Cut eye, nose, and mouth as shown and open out the back.

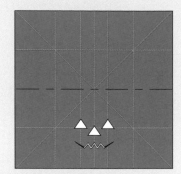

12. Mountain fold in half.

13. Inside reverse folds.

14. Valley fold.

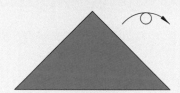

15. Turn over.

16. Valley fold.

17. Valley folds.

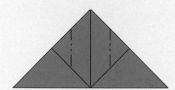

18. Inside reverse folds.

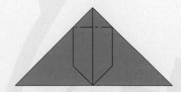

19. Mountain fold.

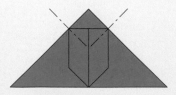

20. Mountain folds.

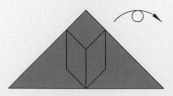

21. Turn over.

22. Valley folds.

23. Inside reverse folds.

24. Mountain fold.

25. Mountain folds.

26. Valley fold.

27. Turn over.

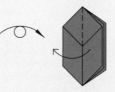

28. Valley fold.

29. Push to pop open.

30. Completed PART 3.

SECOND ASSEMBLY

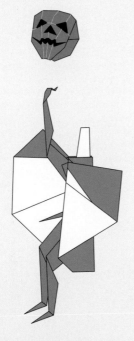

1. Join both parts together as shown and apply glue to hold.

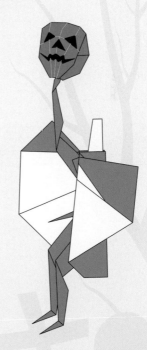

2. Completed SECOND ASSEMBLY.

PART 4

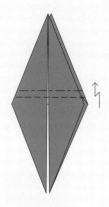

1. Base Fold 3. Pleat fold.

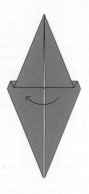

2. Valley fold.

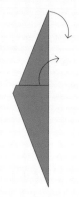

3. Pull and fold.

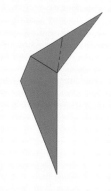

4. Inside reverse fold.

5. Outside reverse fold.

6. Cuts and valley folds.

7. Valley fold.

8. Outside reverse fold front layer.

9. Cut as shown.

10. Outside reverse folds.

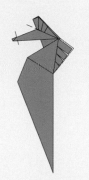

11. Repeat outside reverse folds.

12. Mountain fold.

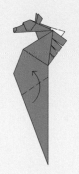

13. Valley fold.

14. Turn over.

15. Valley fold.

✴ **16.** Squash fold.

✴ **17.** Outside reverse fold.

✴ **18.** Inside reverse fold.

✴ **19.** Turn over.

✴ **20.** Squash fold.

✴ **21.** Outside reverse fold.

✴ **22.** Inside reverse fold.

23. Completed PART 4.

PART 5

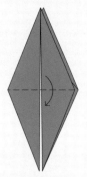

1. Base fold 3.
Valley fold.

2. Turn over.

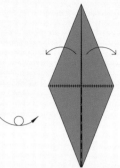

3. Cut through front layer
as shown and valley fold.

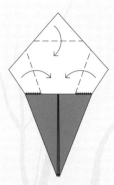

4. Cut as shown
and valley fold.

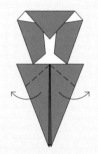

5. Valley folds.

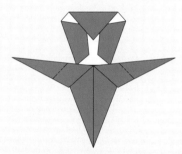

6. Inside reverse folds
then rotate.

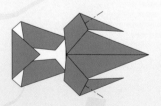

7. Inside reverse folds.

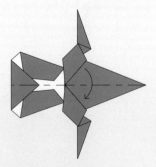

8. Mountain fold in half.

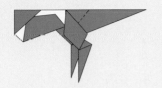

9. Outside reverse fold.

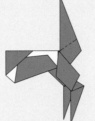

10. Outside reverse fold.

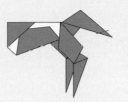

11. Repeat.

12. Completed PART 5.

THIRD ASSEMBLY

1. Join all parts together as shown and apply glue to hold.

2. Completed HEADLESS HORSEMAN.

MUMMY

You'd be cranky too if you were forced to take a 2,000-year nap. No, no, no, he's not trying to rip your face off, he's trying to give you a morning hug!

PART 1

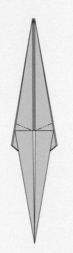

1. Base Fold 4. Valley fold.

2. Inside reverse folds.

3. Cut as shown and valley fold to open out.

4. Valley fold.

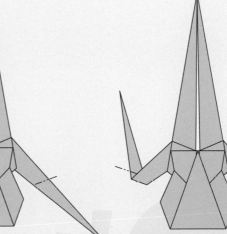

5. Inside reverse folds.

6. Inside reverse folds.

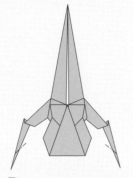

7. Inside reverse folds.

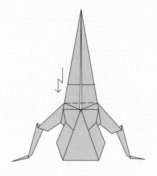

8. Pleat fold.

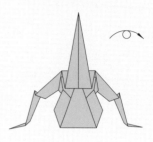

9. Turn over.

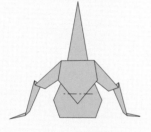

10. Mountain fold.

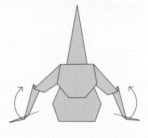

11. Valley folds.

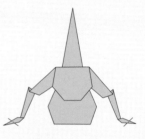

12. Mountain folds.

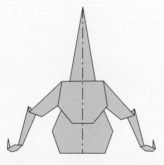

13. Mountain fold in half.

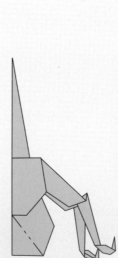

14. Inside reverse fold.

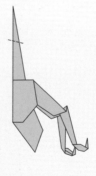

15. Outside reverse fold.

16. Completed PART 1.

PART 2

1. Base Fold 4. Valley fold.

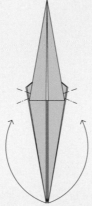

2. Pull and crimp fold at the same time.

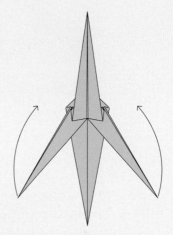

3. Before complete.

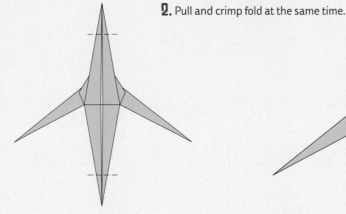

4. Valley folds.

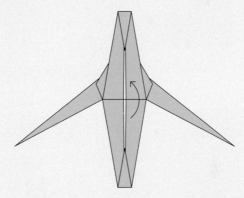

5. Valley fold.

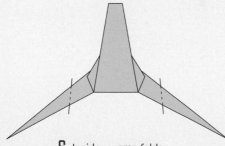

6. Inside reverse folds.

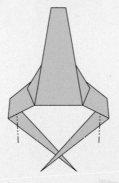

7. Inside reverse folds.

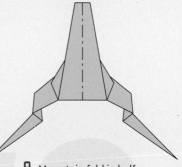

8. Mountain fold in half.

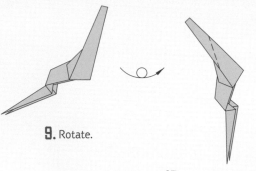

9. Rotate.

10. Outside reverse fold.

11. Outside reverse folds.

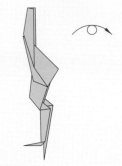

12. Turn over.

13. Outside reverse folds.

14. Completed PART 2.

FIRST ASSEMBLY

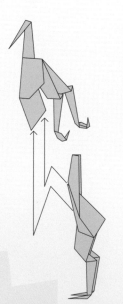
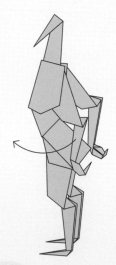
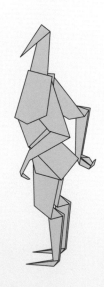

1. Insert in between layers.

2. Pull and fold.

3. Completed FIRST ASSEMBLY.

PART 3

Cut origami paper into a 3.5- by 3.5-inch square.

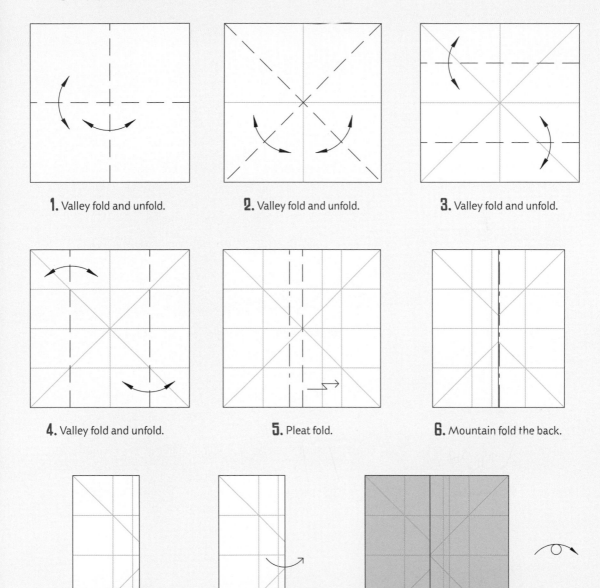

1. Valley fold and unfold.

2. Valley fold and unfold.

3. Valley fold and unfold.

4. Valley fold and unfold.

5. Pleat fold.

6. Mountain fold the back.

7. Cut as shown.

8. Valley fold.

9. Turn over.

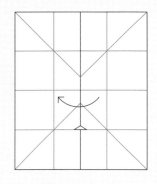

10. Valley fold.

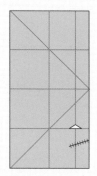

11. Cut as shown.

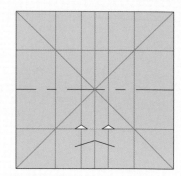

12. Mountain fold in half.

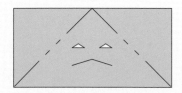

13. Inside reverse folds.

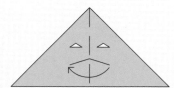

14. Valley fold.

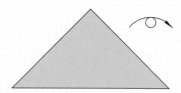

15. Turn over.

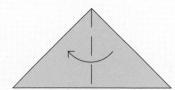

16. Valley fold.

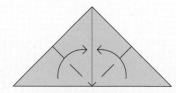

17. Valley folds.

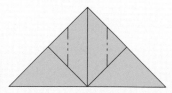

18. Inside reverse folds.

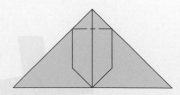

19. Mountain fold.

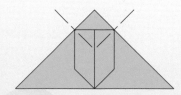

20. Mountain folds.

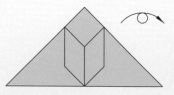

21. Turn over.

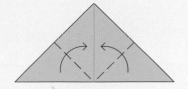

22. Valley folds.

23. Inside reverse folds.

24. Mountain fold.

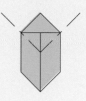

25. Mountain folds.

26. Valley fold.

27. Turn over.

28. Valley fold.

29. Push to pop open.

30. Completed PART 3.

SECOND ASSEMBLY

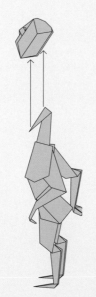

1. Glue Part 3 to body as shown.

2. Turn head to front.

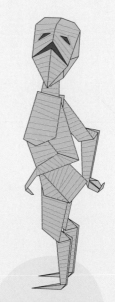

3. Completed MUMMY.

SCARECROW

A group of crows is called a murder.
A group of scarecrows is called an apocalypse.

PART 1

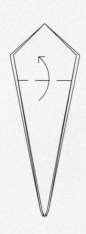

1. Base Fold 4. Valley fold.

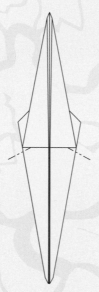

2. Inside reverse folds.

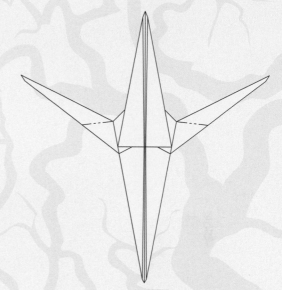

3. Inside reverse folds.

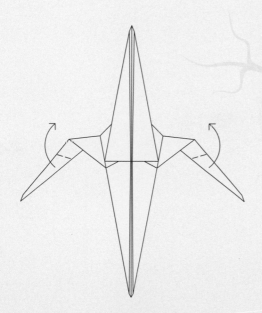

4. Valley folds.

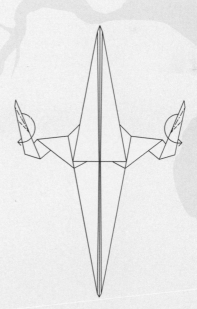

5. Valley folds.

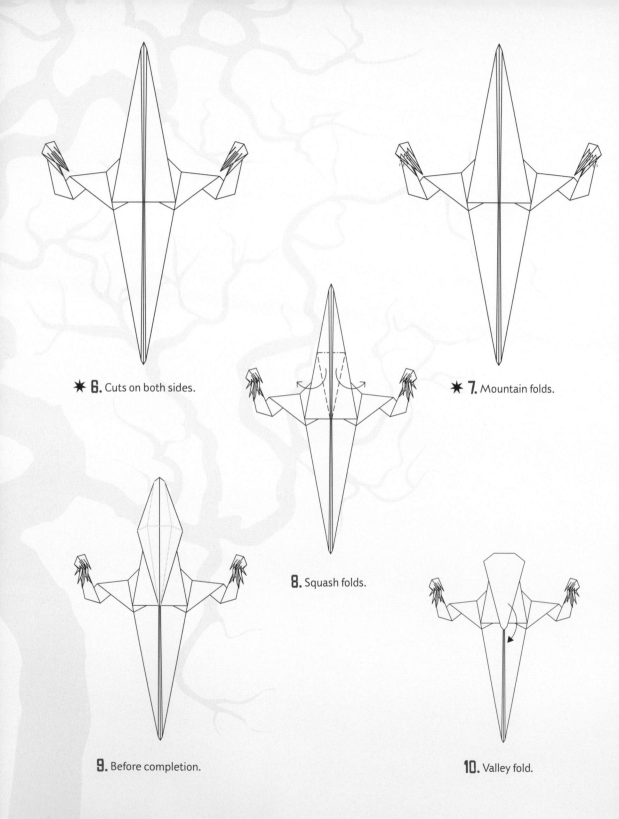

✹ **6.** Cuts on both sides.

✹ **7.** Mountain folds.

8. Squash folds.

9. Before completion.

10. Valley fold.

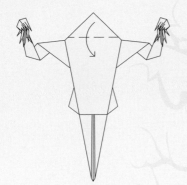

11. Valley fold.

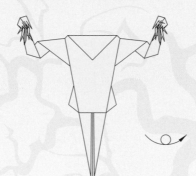

12. Turn over.

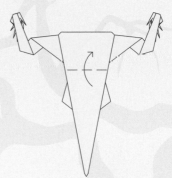

13. Valley fold.

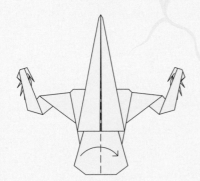

14. Valley fold.

15. Crimp fold.

16. Inside reverse fold.

17. Outside reverse fold.

18. Flatten.

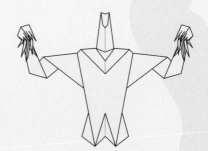

19. Completed PART 1.

PART 2

1. Base Fold 4. Valley fold.

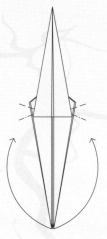

2. Pull and crimp folds at the same time.

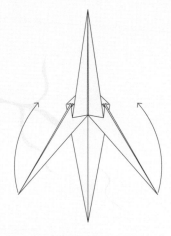

3. Before complete.

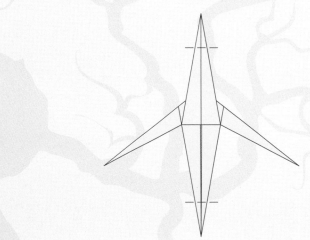

4. Valley folds.

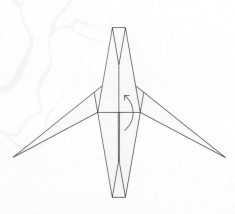

5. Valley fold.

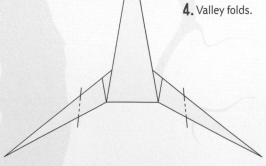

6. Inside reverse folds.

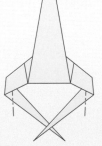

7. Inside reverse folds.

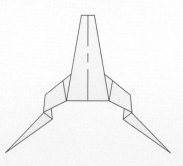

8. Mountain fold in half.

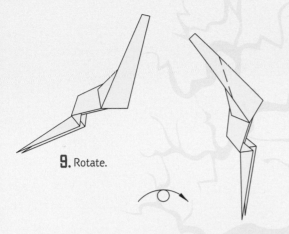

9. Rotate.

10. Outside reverse fold.

11. Outside reverse folds.

12. Completed PART 2.

FIRST ASSEMBLY

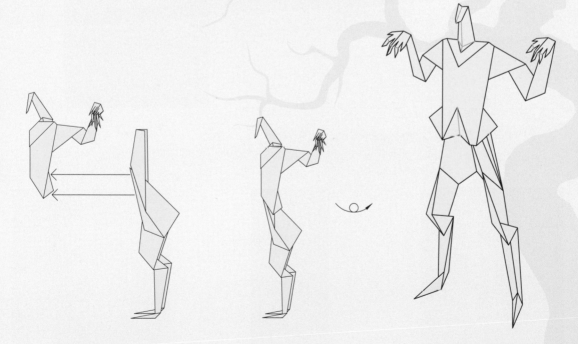

1. Insert as shown, apply glue to hold and turn to the front.

2. Completed FIRST ASSEMBLY.

PART 3

Cut origami paper into a 3.5- by 3.5-inch square.

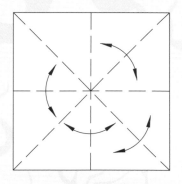

1. Valley fold and unfold.

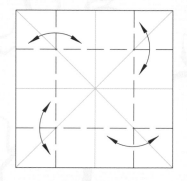

2. Valley fold and unfold.

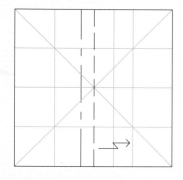

3. Pleat fold.

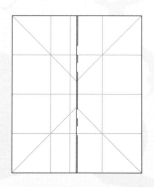

4. Mountain fold.

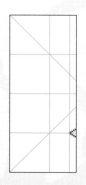

5. Cut as shown.

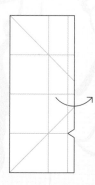

6. Valley fold.

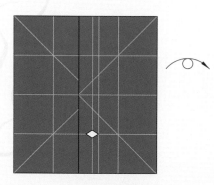

7. Turn over.

8. Valley fold.

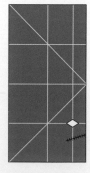

9. Cut and flatten.

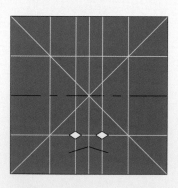

10. Mountain fold in half.

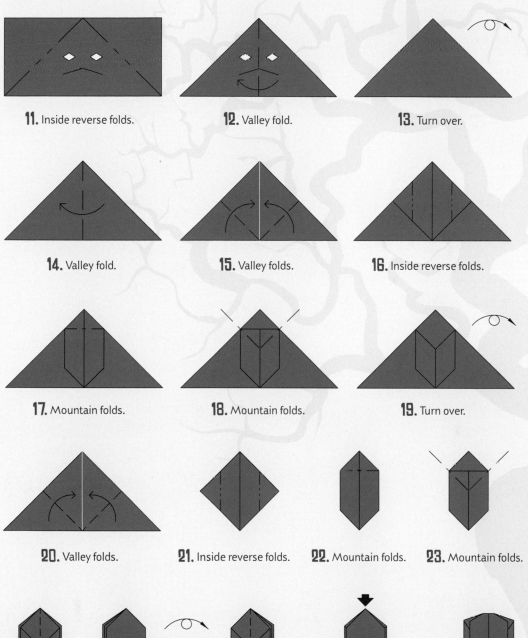

11. Inside reverse folds.

12. Valley fold.

13. Turn over.

14. Valley fold.

15. Valley folds.

16. Inside reverse folds.

17. Mountain folds.

18. Mountain folds.

19. Turn over.

20. Valley folds.

21. Inside reverse folds.

22. Mountain folds.

23. Mountain folds.

24. Valley fold.

25. Turn over.

26. Valley fold.

27. Push to pop open.

28. Completed PART 3.

PART 4

Cut origami paper into a 4- by 4-inch square.

1. Start with Base Fold 2. Fold and unfold.

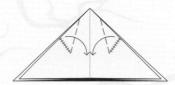

2. Cuts and valley folds.

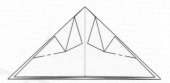

3. Mountain folds.

4. Inside reverse folds.

5. Crimp fold at the center.

6. Turn over.

7. Cuts and valley folds.

8. Mountain folds.

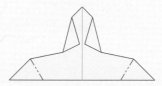

9. Inside reverse folds.

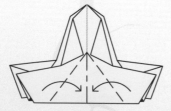

10. Crimp fold at the center.

11. Valley fold to open flaps.

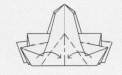 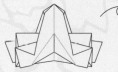  

12. Crimp fold at the center.　　**13.** Turn over.　　**14.** Crimp fold at the center.　　**15.** Completed PART 4.

SECOND ASSEMBLY

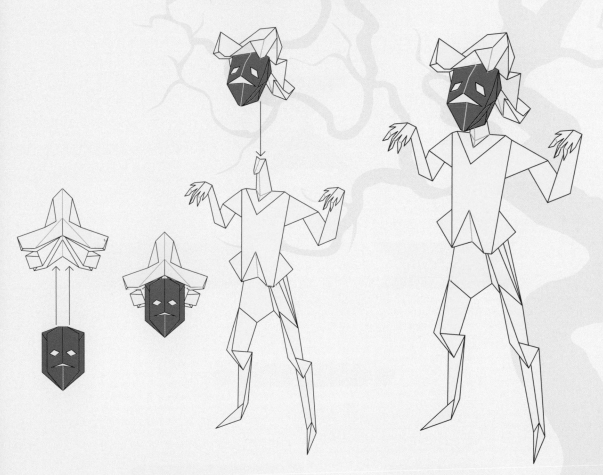

1. Join all parts together as indicated by the arrows and apply glue to hold.

2. Completed SECOND ASSEMBLY.

PART 5

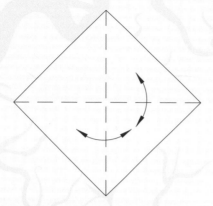

1. Valley fold and unfold.

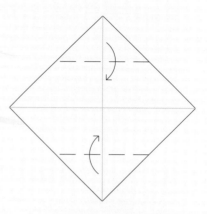

2. Valley folds.

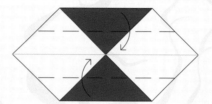

3. Valley folds.

4. Turn over.

5. Valley folds.

6. Valley fold in half.

7. Valley fold the front.

8. Turn over.

9. Valley fold.

10. Make another for the final assembly.

11. Completed PART 5 and PART 6.

FINAL ASSEMBLY

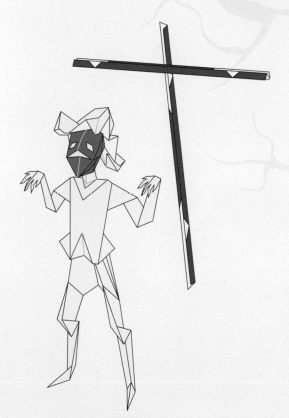

1. Join all parts together as shown and apply glue to hold.

2. Completed SCARECROW.

WITCH

Sugar and spice and everything nice, that's what little girls are made of. This witch's brew is made of little girls. It's important to know where your food comes from.

PART 1

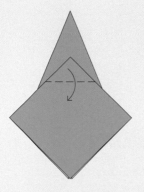

1. Step 7 of Base Fold 3. Valley fold.

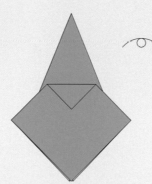

2. Turn over.

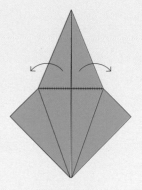

3. Cuts and valley folds.

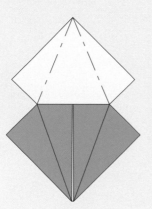

4. Mountain folds.

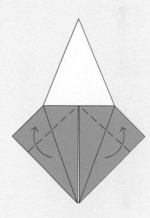

5. Valley folds.

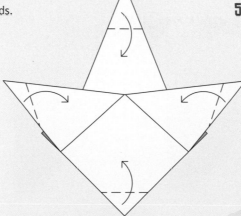

6. Valley folds.

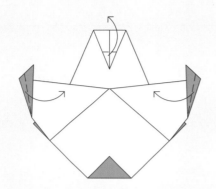

7. Valley folds.

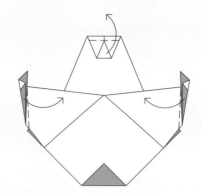

8. Valley folds.

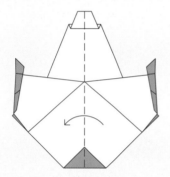

9. Valley fold in half.

10. Tuck in or hide the neck layers behind the hood area of the cape.

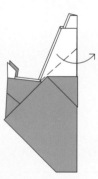

11. Valley fold.

12. Squash fold.

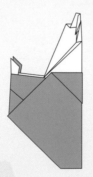

13. Before complete.

14. Valley folds.

15. Completed PART 1.

PART 2

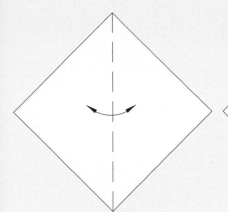

1. Valley fold and unfold.

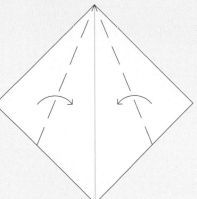

2. Valley folds.

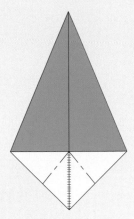

3. Cut and mountain folds.

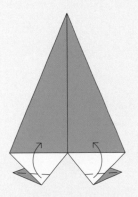

4. Valley folds.

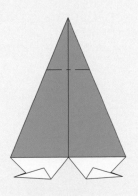

5. Mountain fold.

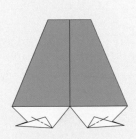

6. Mountain folds.

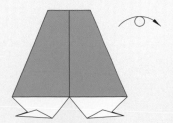

7. Turn over.

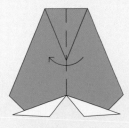

8. Valley fold.

9. Completed PART 2.

PART 3

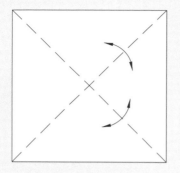

1. Valley folds and unfold.

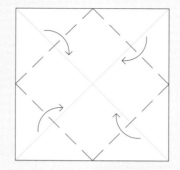

2. Valley folds.

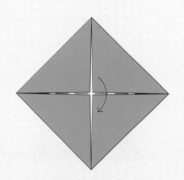

3. Valley fold.

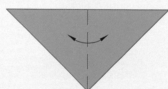

4. Valley fold and unfold.

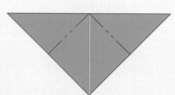

5. Inside reverse folds.

6. Scale-up.

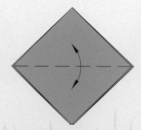

7. Valley fold and unfold.

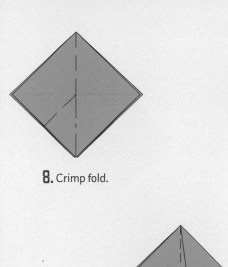

8. Crimp fold.

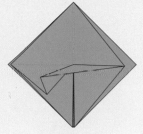

9. Before complete.

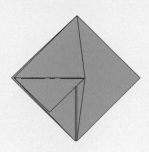

10. Mountain fold.

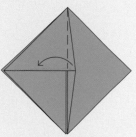

11. Valley fold.

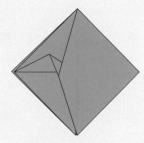

12. Before complete.

13. Turn over.

14. Valley fold.

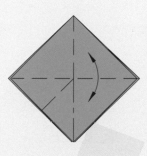

15. Repeat steps 7 to 10.

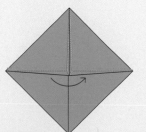

16. Valley fold.

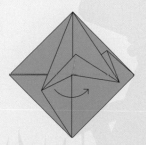

17. Before complete.

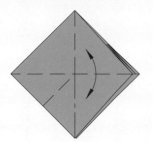

18. Repeat steps 7–10.

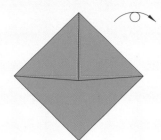

19. Turn over.

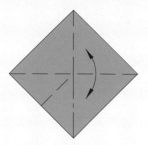

20. Repeat steps 7–10.

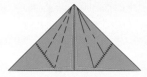

21. Cuts, valley and mountain folds.

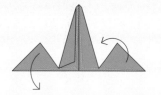

22. Valley and mountain fold.

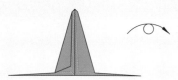

23. Turn over.

24. Repeat steps 22 and 23.

25. Valley fold.

26. Rotate.

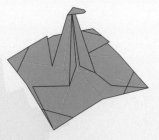

27. Mountain folds.

28. Completed PART 3.

ASSEMBLY

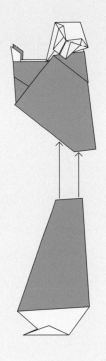

1. Insert in between layers.

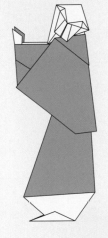

2. Place hat and apply glue.

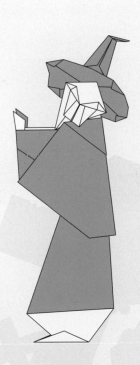

3. Completed WITCH.

WOLF MAN

HAIRY AND SCARY! He's like the Wolverine,
only deadlier and with more fleas.

PART 1

1. Valley fold and unfold.

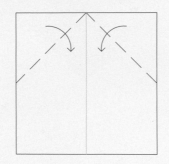

2. Valley folds.

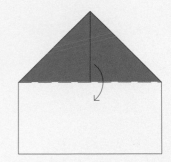

3. Valley fold.

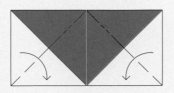

4. Valley and inside reverse folds.

5. Turn over.

6. Valley fold.

7. Valley fold.

8. Unfold.

9. Crimp fold.

10. Valley fold.

11. Valley fold.

12. Unfold.

13. Crimp fold.

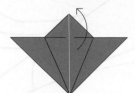

14. Valley fold.

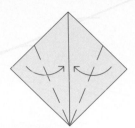

15. Valley folds.

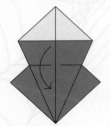

16. Valley fold.

17. Unfold inner layers.

18. Turn over.

19. Scale-up.

20. Valley fold.

21. Inside reverse folds.

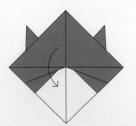

22. Valley fold.

23. Valley and squash folds.

24. Valley folds.

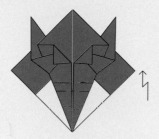

25. Pleat fold.

26. Valley fold.

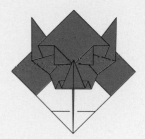

27. Valley fold.

28. Turn over.

29. Valley fold.

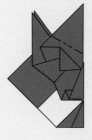

30. Inside reverse fold.

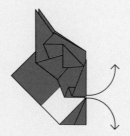

31. Pull and fold.

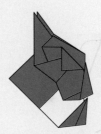

32. Flatten.

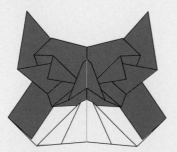

33. Completed PART 1.

PART 2

1. Base Fold 3. Turn upside down. Inside reverse fold.

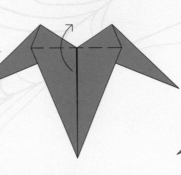

2. Valley fold both sides.

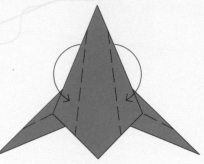

3. Squash folds.

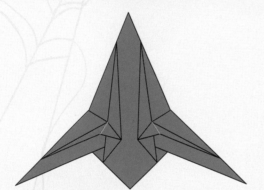

4. Before complete.

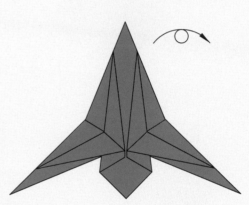

5. Turn over.

6. Squash folds.

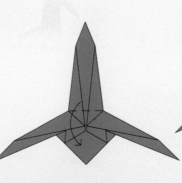

7. Valley fold.

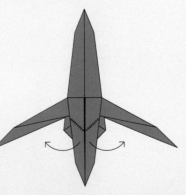

8. Cut the front and valley fold out the cut parts.

9. Before complete.

10. Pleat fold.

11. Cuts as shown.

12. Valley folds.

13. Crimp folds.

14. Valley fold.

15. Outside reverse fold.

16. Inside reverse fold.

17. Pleat fold both sides.

18. Completed PART 2.

PART 3

1. Base Fold 4. Valley fold.

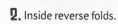

2. Inside reverse folds.

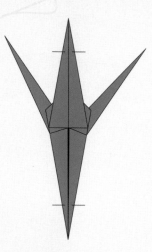

3. Valley folds.

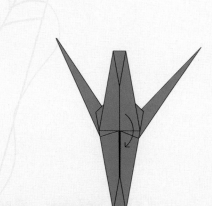

4. Valley fold.

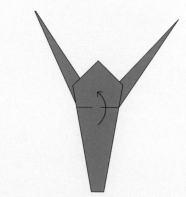

5. Valley fold.

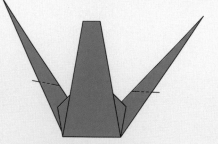

6. Inside reverse folds.

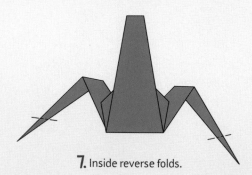

7. Inside reverse folds.

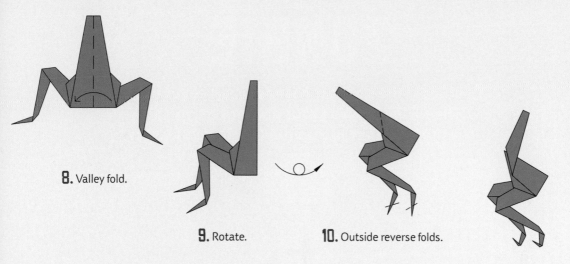

8. Valley fold.

9. Rotate.

10. Outside reverse folds.

11. Completed PART 3.

ASSEMBLY

1. Insert all parts together as shown and apply glue to hold.

2. Completed WOLF MAN.

ZOMBIE

Zombies make the best friends. They never argue.
They'll follow you around wherever you go.
The only problem is that they're always hungry.

PART 1

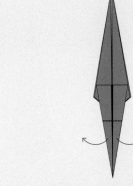

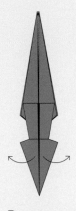

1. Base Fold 4. Valley fold.

2. Cut and valley fold out.

3. Valley fold out.

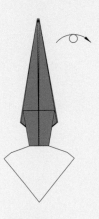

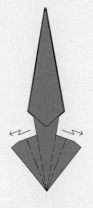

4. Turn over.

5. Pleat folds.

6. Valley folds.

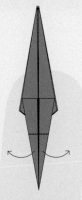

7. Cuts as shown.

8. Valley fold.

9. Repeat steps 2 to 7.

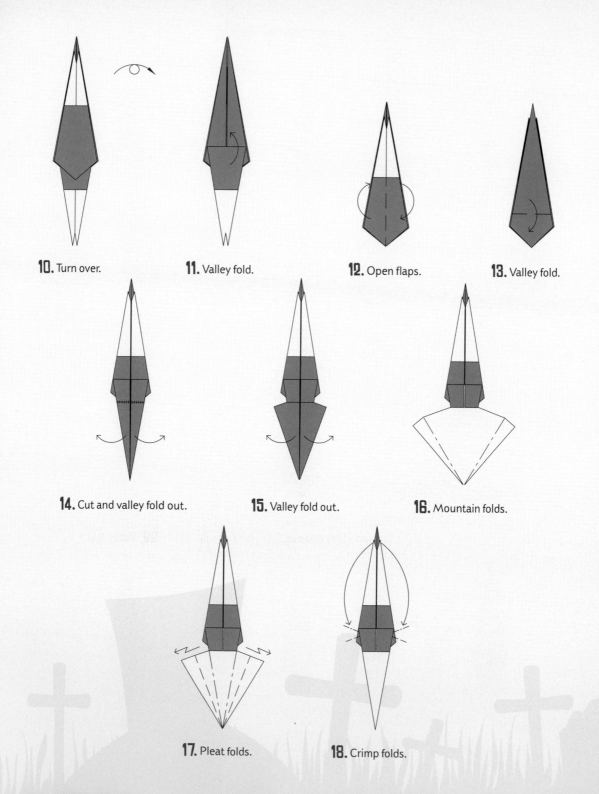

10. Turn over.

11. Valley fold.

12. Open flaps.

13. Valley fold.

14. Cut and valley fold out.

15. Valley fold out.

16. Mountain folds.

17. Pleat folds.

18. Crimp folds.

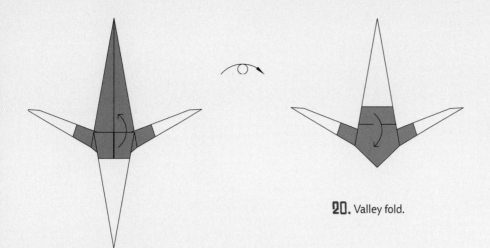

19. Valley fold and turn over.

20. Valley fold.

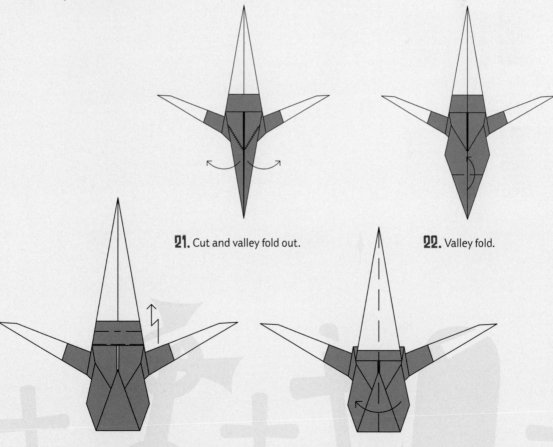

21. Cut and valley fold out.

22. Valley fold.

23. Pleat fold.

24. Valley fold in half.

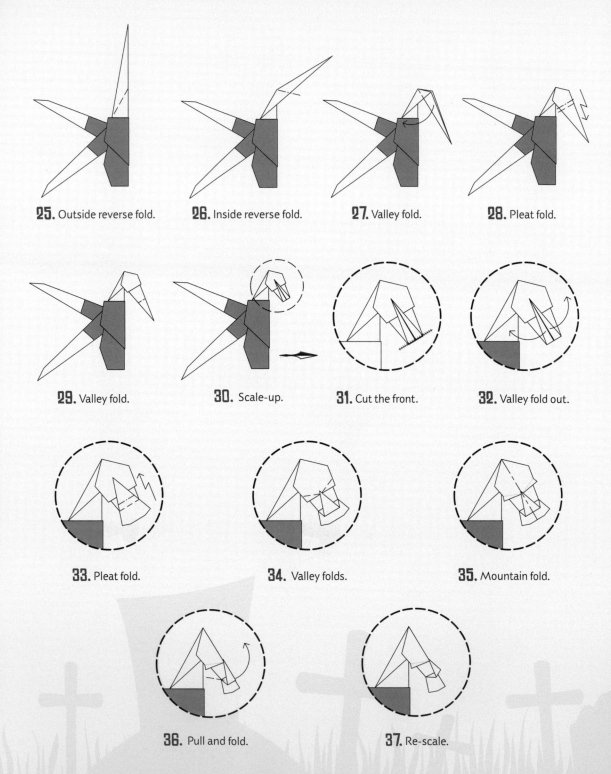

25. Outside reverse fold.

26. Inside reverse fold.

27. Valley fold.

28. Pleat fold.

29. Valley fold.

30. Scale-up.

31. Cut the front.

32. Valley fold out.

33. Pleat fold.

34. Valley folds.

35. Mountain fold.

36. Pull and fold.

37. Re-scale.

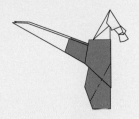

38. Inside reverse fold.

39. Cut and valley fold.

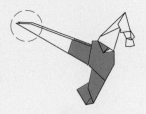

✴ **40.** Scale-up.

✴ **41.** Mountain fold.

✴ **42.** Repeat.

✴ **43.** Mountain fold.

✴ **44.** Repeat.

✴ **45.** Re-scale.

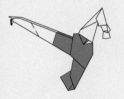

46. Valley fold.

47. Valley fold.

48. Turn over.

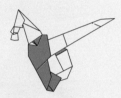

49. Mountain fold.

50. Valley fold.

51. Valley fold.

52. Flatten.

53. Flatten.

54. Flatten.

PART 2

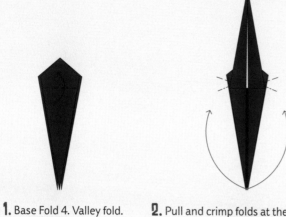
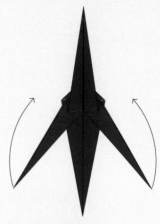

1. Base Fold 4. Valley fold.

2. Pull and crimp folds at the same time.

3. Before complete.

4. Valley folds.

5. Valley fold.

6. Inside reverse folds.

7. Valley folds.

8. Valley folds.

9. Valley folds.

✳ **10.** Inside reverse fold.

✳ **11.** Mountain fold.

✳ **12.** Mountain fold.

✳ **13.** Outside reverse fold.

✳ **14.** Flatten.

✳ **15.** Completed PART 2.

ASSEMBLY

1. Insert Part 2 in between layers of Part 1 where the arrows indicate.

2. Completed ZOMBIE.

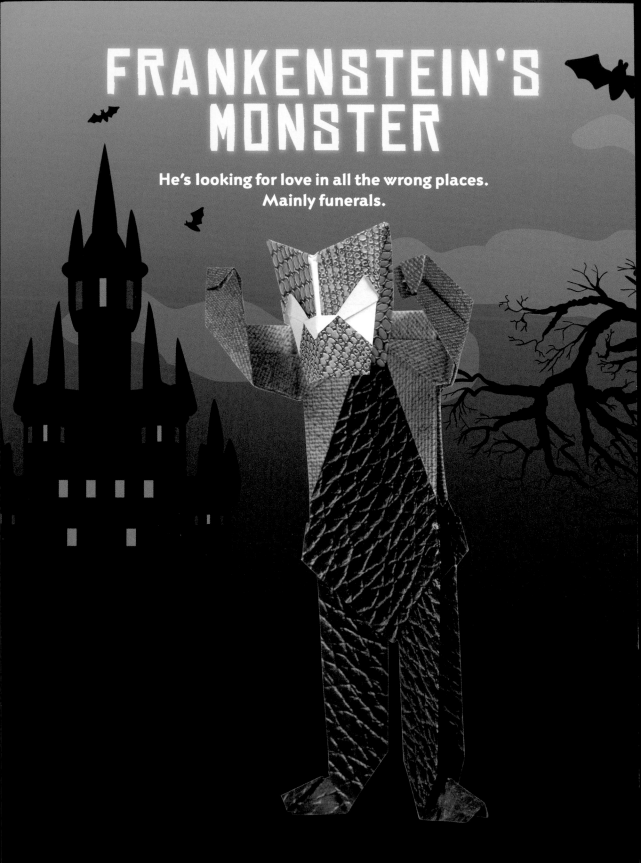

FRANKENSTEIN'S MONSTER

He's looking for love in all the wrong places.
Mainly funerals.

PART 1

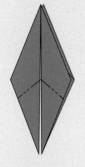

1. Start with Base Fold 3. Inside reverse folds.

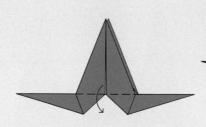

2. Valley fold.

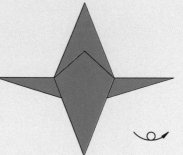

3. Turn over.

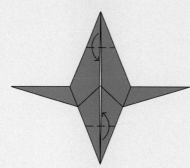

4. Valley folds.

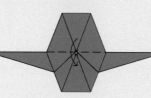

5. Valley fold.

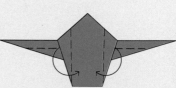

6. Valley folds and squash folds at the same time. Repeat on the other side.

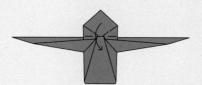

7. Valley fold.

8. Turn over.

9. Valley folds.

10. Valley folds.

11. Cut as shown.

12. Completed PART I.

PART 2

1. Base Fold 4. Rotate.

2. Valley fold both sides.

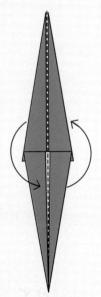

3. Valley folds to open flaps.

4. Valley fold.

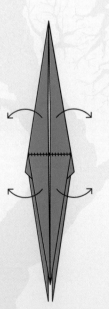

5. Cut and open folds outward.

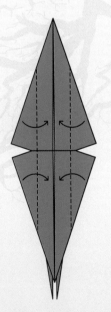

6. Valley folds.

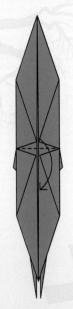

7. Valley fold.

8. Slide flap into slot.

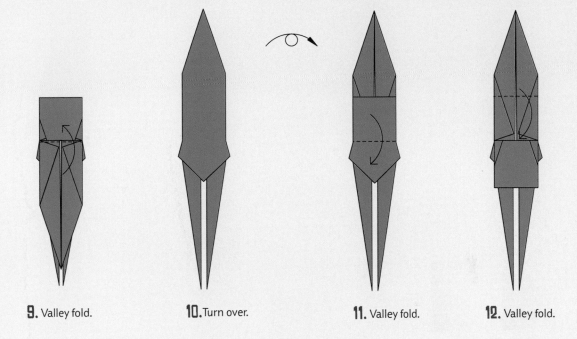

9. Valley fold.

10. Turn over.

11. Valley fold.

12. Valley fold.

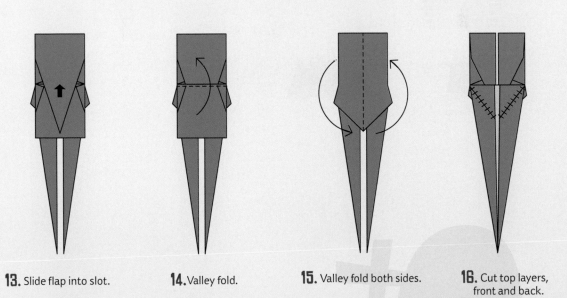

13. Slide flap into slot.

14. Valley fold.

15. Valley fold both sides.

16. Cut top layers, front and back.

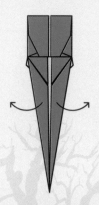

17. Valley open cut parts, front and back.

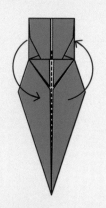

18. Valley fold both sides to open flaps.

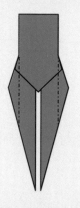

19. Mountain fold top layers.

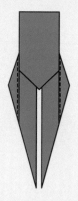

20. Valley folds.

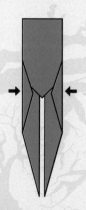

21. Hide flaps between layers.

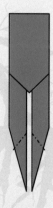

22. Inside reverse folds.

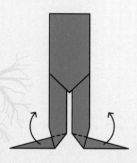

23. Valley fold top layers.

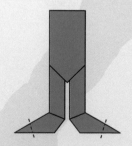

24. Mountain folds.

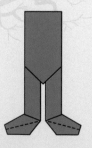

25. Valley folds.

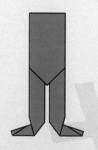

26. Add coloring.

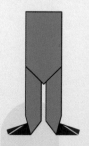

27. Completed PART 2.

PART 3

Cut origami paper into a 2.5- by 2.5-inch square.

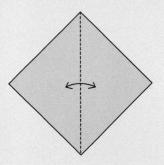

1. Valley fold and unfold.

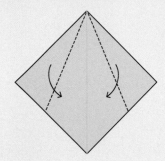

2. Valley folds.

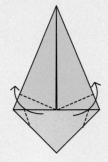

3. Crimp folds.

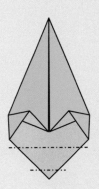

4. Pleat fold.

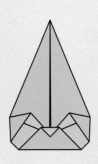

5. Turn over.

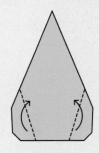

6. Valley folds.

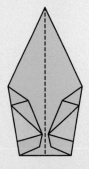

7. Valley fold in half.

8. Inside reverse fold.

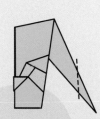

9. Outside reverse fold.

10. Add color to both sides.

11. Open out forward.

12. Completed PART 3.

ASSEMBLY

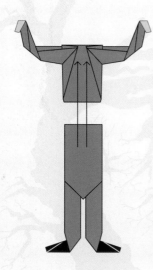

1. Insert part 2 into part 1 as shown, and apply glue to hold.

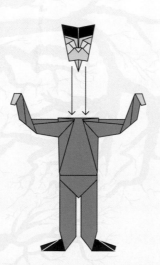

2. Position part 3 (head) onto body. Open folds to stand.

3. Completed FRANKENSTEIN'S MONSTER.

CREATURE FROM THE BLACK LAGOON

Ahoy matey! A life jacket won't save you from this baddie.
If you don't have a harpoon with a rocket launcher attached,
you're going to be swimming with the fishes.

PART 1

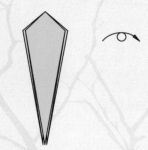

1. Start with Base Fold 4. Rotate.

2. Valley fold.

3. Inside reverse fold.

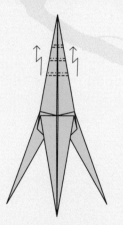

4. Pleat folds.

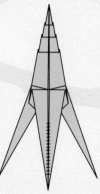

5. Cut as shown.

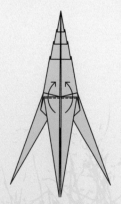

6. Valley fold.

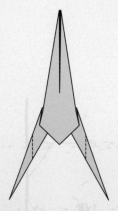

7. Outside reverse folds.

8. Valley fold.

9. See close-ups for more details.

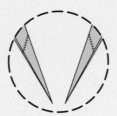

10. Cuts to top layers, front and back.

11. Valley fold to open out, front and back.

12. Cuts to top layers, front and back.

13. Valley fold to open out, front and back.

14. Outside reverse folds.

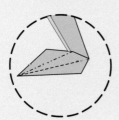

15. Pleat fold right side loosely, front and back.

16. Pleat completed.

17. Repeat pleat fold on left side, front and back.

18. Back to full view.

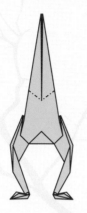

19. Mountain folds.

20. Valley fold.

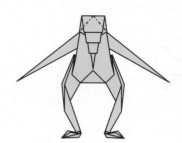

21. Mountain folds.

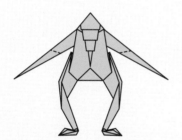

22. Valley folds.

23. Valley folds.

24. Inside reverse folds.

25. Valley folds, to
position forward.

26. Inside reverse folds,
to open body.

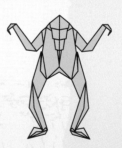

27. Completed PART 1.

PART 2

Cut origami paper into a 3- by 3-inch square.

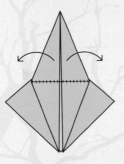

1. Start with step 7 of Base Fold 3. Cut and valley fold to open out.

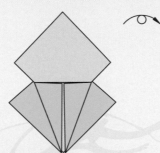

2. Turn over.

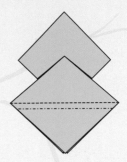

3. Pleat fold.

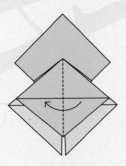

4. Valley fold.

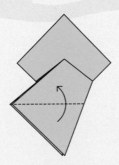

5. Valley fold.

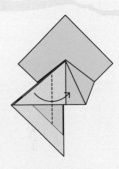

6. Valley fold.

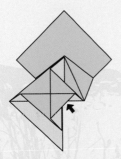

7. Hide flap behind layer.

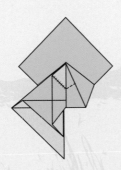

8. Cut as shown and valley fold.

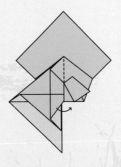

9. Valley fold top layer.

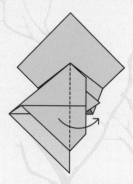

10. Valley fold.

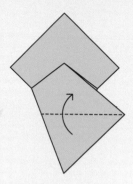

11. Valley fold.

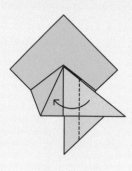

12. Valley fold.

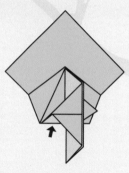

13. Hide flap behind layer.

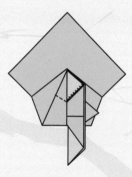

14. Cut as shown and valley fold.

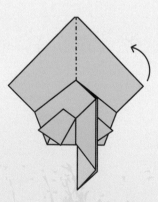

15. Mountain fold back layer.

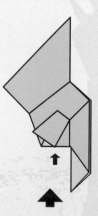

16. Push to open, and rotate to front

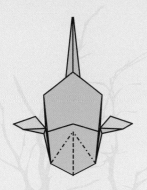

17. Inside reverse fold.

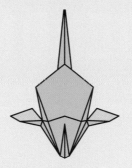

18. Attach "eyes" with glue.

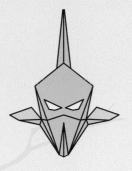

19. Completed PART 2.

ASSEMBLY

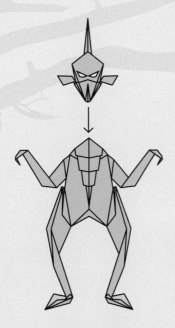

1. Join parts together as shown and apply glue to hold.

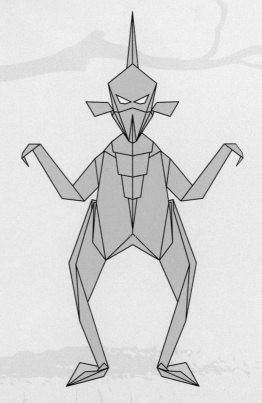

2. Completed CREATURE FROM THE BLACK LAGOON.

PART 1

1. Start with Base Fold 3. Inside reverse folds.

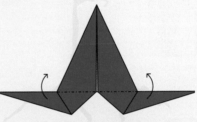

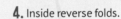

2. Valley and squash folds at same time.

3. Turn over.

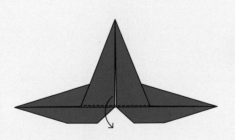

4. Inside reverse folds.

5. Valley fold.

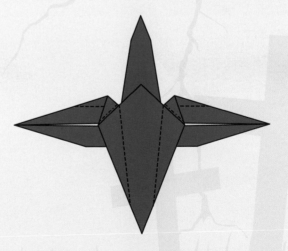

6. Valley and squash folds at same time.

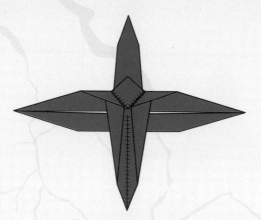

7. Make cuts as shown.

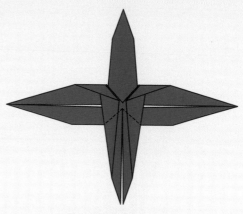

8. Valley fold both sides.

9. Turn over.

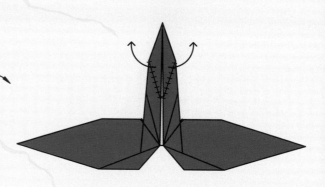

10. Cut top layer only, valley fold open the cut parts.

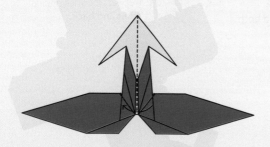

11. Valley fold in half.

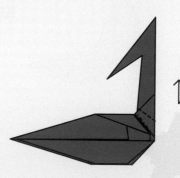

12. Crimp fold.

13. Outside reverse fold.

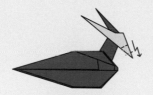

14. Pleat fold.

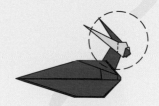

✱ **15.** Valley fold both sides. See close-ups for details.

✱ **16.** Mountain fold both sides.

✱ **17.** Repeat mountain folds both sides.

✱ **18.** Back to full view.

19. Valley fold both sides.

20. Mountain fold both front and back.

21. Repeat, mountain folds front and back.

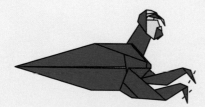

22. Again, mountain folds front and back.

23. Completed PART 1.

PART 2

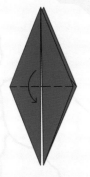

1. Start with Base Fold 3. Valley fold.

2. Turn over.

3. Valley folds.

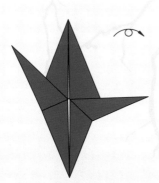

4. Turn over.

5. Valley and squash fold both sides. Inside reverse fold.

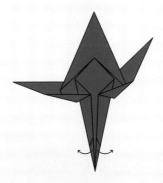

6. Cut and valley fold out the cut parts.

7. Valley fold in half. Rotate.

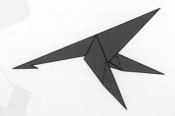

8. Inside reverse folds.

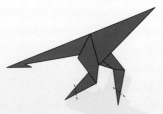

9. Inside reverse folds.

10. See close-ups for more detail.

11. Inside reverse folds.

✳ **12.** Cut edges to separate. Back to full view.

13. Inside reverse fold.

14. Inside reverse fold.

15. Mountain fold.

16. Completed PART 2.

PARTS 3 AND 4

Cut origami paper into a 3- by 3-inch square.

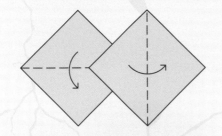

1. Valley fold two squares.

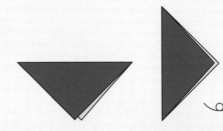

2. Rotate one sheet as shown.

3. Insert rotated sheet between layers as shown.

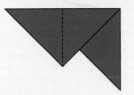

4. Valley fold. (Mountain fold for PART 4.)

5. Turn over for PART 3 only.

PART 3

6. Valley fold, allowing back flap to come forward.

7. Valley fold flap.

8. Open and rotate forward.

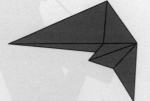

9. Completed PART 3.

PART 4

6. Valley fold, allowing back flap to come forward.

7. Valley fold flap.

8. Open and rotate forward.

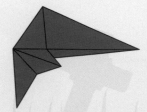

9. Completed PART 4.

ASSEMBLY

1. Join parts 1 and 2 and apply glue to hold.

2. Insert wings into slots, and secure with glue.

3. Valley fold inner wings, both sides.

4. Completed DEMON.

THREE-HEADED DRAGON

If you meet this fire breather, do NOT think, "how to train my dragon," think, "how to SLAY my dragon." He does not want to be your cuddly sidekick. He wants you to be his crispy midnight snack.

PART 1

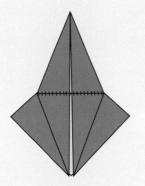

1. Start with step 7 of Base Fold 3. Cut as shown.

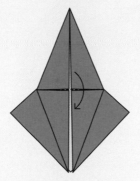

2. Valley fold.

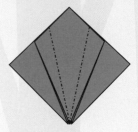

3. Inside reverse folds.

4. Turn over.

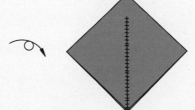

5. Cut as shown.

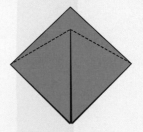

6. Valley fold cut parts.

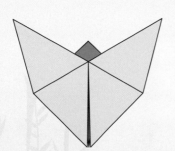

7. Turn over.

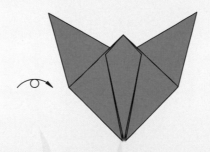

8. Rotate.

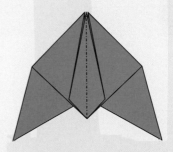

9. Mountain fold in half.

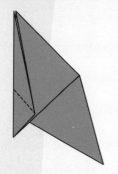

10. Outside reverse fold.

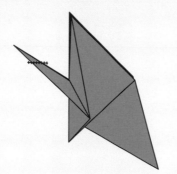

11. Cut front layers, both sides.

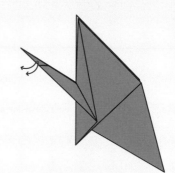

12. Open out cut parts.

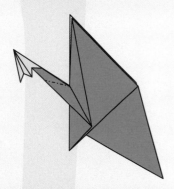

13. Inside reverse fold.

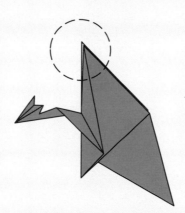

✱ **14.** See close-ups for detail.

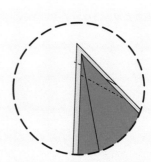

✱ **15.** Mountain fold front and back.

✱ **16.** Valley fold front and back.

✱ **17.** Outside reverse folds.

✱ **18.** Back to full view.

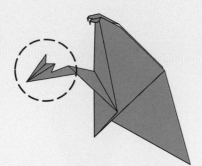

19. See close-ups for detail.

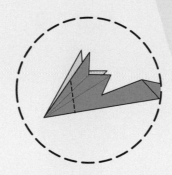

20. Outside reverse folds.

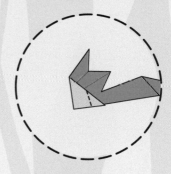

21. Outside reverse folds.

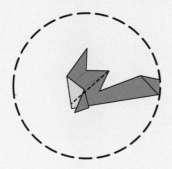

22. Valley fold both sides.

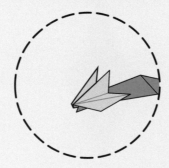

23. Back to full view.

24. Valley fold outward, both sides.

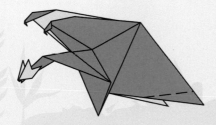

25. Valley folds, front and back.

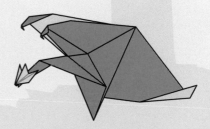

26. Completed PART 1.

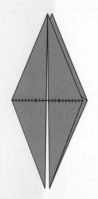

PART 2

1. Start with Base Fold 3. Cut front layers only as shown.

2. Valley fold.

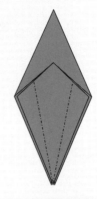

3. Inside reverse folds.

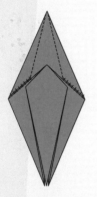

4. Cuts and valley folds.

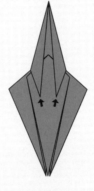

5. Hide flaps behind layers.

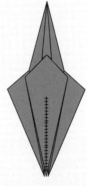

6. Cut as shown.

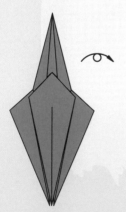

7. Turn over.

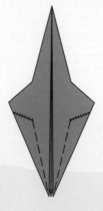

8. Cuts and valley folds.

9. Valley fold in half.

10. Rotate.

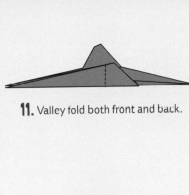

11. Valley fold both front and back.

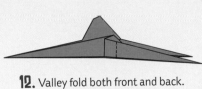

12. Valley fold both front and back.

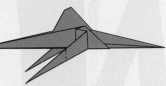

13. Inside reverse fold both sides.

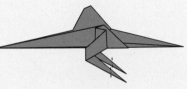

14. Repeat.

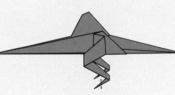

15. Repeat.

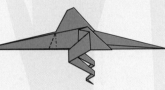

16. Crimp fold both sides.

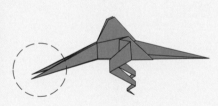

17. See close-ups for detail.

18. Cuts to all four sides.

19. Open out cut parts.

20. Outside reverse folds.

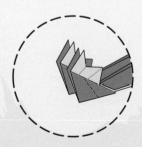

21. Repeat outside reverse folds.

22. Valley fold all sides.

23. Back to full view.

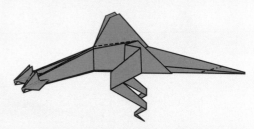

24. Inside reverse fold tail and valley folds to both sides.

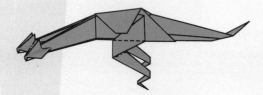

25. Hide flaps, and pleat fold loosely to position "legs."

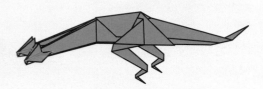

26. Completed PART 2.

ASSEMBLY

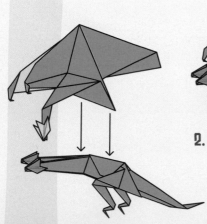

1. Join both parts together as shown and apply glue to hold.

2. Valley fold heads aside to separate.

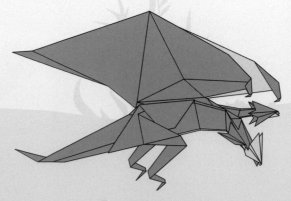

3. Completed DRAGON.

DRACULA

Super strength. Invincible. Lives forever. Vampires are always terrifying. But the king of the vampires? Blood curdling . . . which, coincidentally, is his favorite type of smoothie.

PART 1

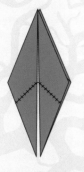

1. Start with Base Fold 3. Cut as shown.

2. Valley folds.

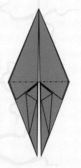

3. Mountain fold lower flaps to inside.

4. Valley open flap.

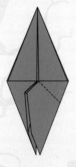

5. Valley fold.

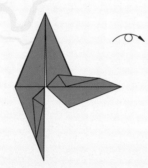

6. Turn over.

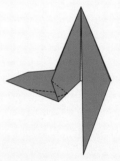

7. Valley fold and squash fold at same time.

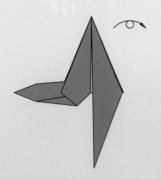

8. Turn over.

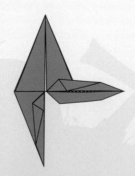

9. Valley fold.

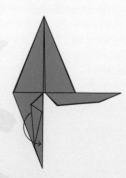

10. Valley open out.

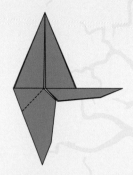

11. Valley fold.

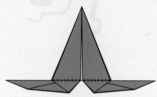

12. Turn over.

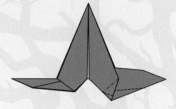

13. Valley fold and squash fold at same time.

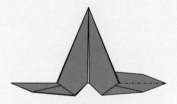
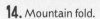

14. Mountain fold.

15. Cut as shown.

16. Valley fold to open out the cut parts.

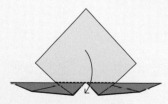

17. Valley fold.

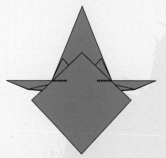

18. Cuts as shown.

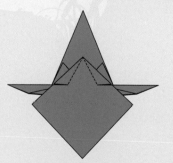

19. Valley fold cut parts.

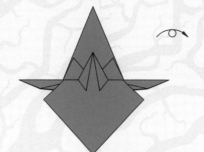

20. Turn over.

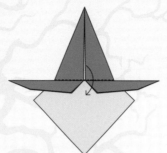

21. Valley fold.

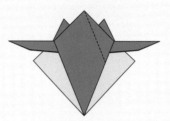

22. Valley fold.

23. Valley fold.

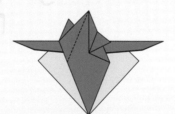

24. Valley fold.

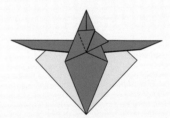

25. Valley fold.

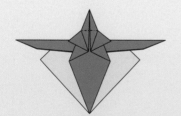

26. Mountain fold.

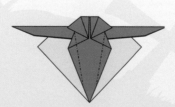

27. Mountain folds.

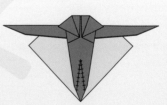

28. Cut as shown.

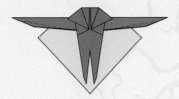

29. Mountain fold front layers.

30. Valley fold back layers.

31. Hide flaps between layers.

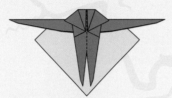

32. Pull top layers forward and valley to open body.

33. Completed PART I.

PART 2

1. Start with Base Fold 5. Valley fold.

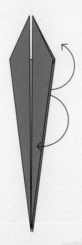

2. Open flaps.

3. Valley fold.

4. Valley fold.

5. Valley fold.

6. Valley fold.

7. Valley fold.

8. Valley fold front layer.

9. Inside reverse folds.

10. Valley fold to open form.

11. Completed PART 2.

PART 3

Cut origami paper into a 3- by 3-inch square.

1. Start with Base Fold 3. Cut as shown, front and back.

2. Valley fold to open, front and back.

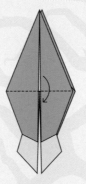

3. Valley fold.

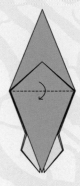

4. Valley fold.

5. Pleat fold.

6. Cut as shown.

7. Pull open and squash fold.

8. Valley fold.

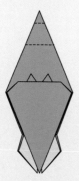

9. Valley folds.

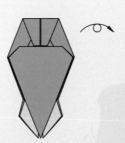

10. Rotate.

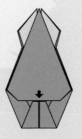

11. Hide flap behind front layer.

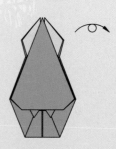

12. Turn over.

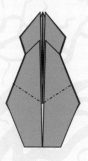

13. Inside reverse folds.

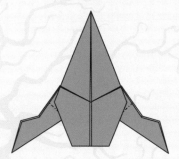

14. Inside reverse folds.

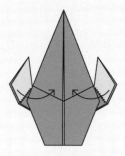

15. Cut top layer and valley open.

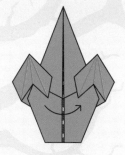

16. Valley fold in half.

17. Inside reverse fold.

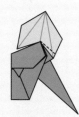

18. Valley fold both sides.

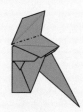

19. Mountain fold both sides.

20. Open out and turn forward.

21. Add coloring and detail.

22. Completed PART 3.

ASSEMBLY

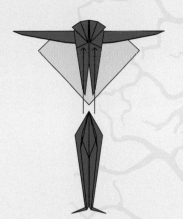

1. Join parts 1 and 2 together as shown. Glue to hold.

2. Valley fold.

3. Mountain fold.

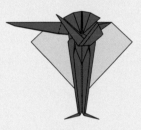

4. Repeat steps 2 and 3 on other side.

5. Valley folds.

6. Mountain folds, and add detail and coloring.

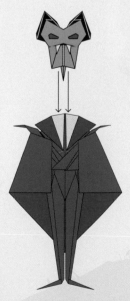

7. Position part 3 and apply glue.

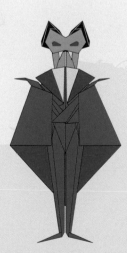

8. Completed DRACULA.

ALIEN

In space, no one can hear you scream. But they can hear you frantically calling NASA for help. With a monster this scary, don't be surprised if no one answers.

PART 1

1. Start with Base Fold 4. Rotate.

2. Valley fold.

3. Inside reverse folds.

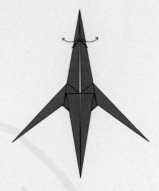

4. Cut and valley fold to open.

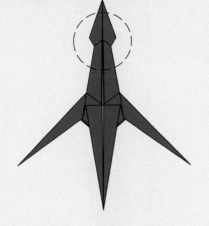

5. See close-ups for detail.

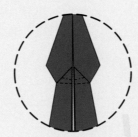

6. Pleat folds.

7. Back to full view.

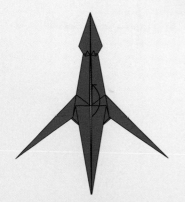

8. Valley fold.

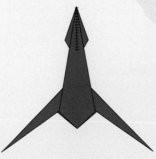

9. Cut as shown.

10. Inside reverse folds.

11. Inside reverse folds.

12. Inside reverse folds.

13. Inside reverse folds.

14. Mountain fold in half.

15. Crimp fold.

16. Valley fold both sides.

17. Outside reverse folds.

18. Outside reverse fold.

19. Outside reverse fold.

20. Mountain fold both sides down middle.

21. Mountain fold both sides and wrap to inside.

22. Completed PART 1.

PART 2

1. Start with Base Fold 4. Valley fold.

2. Inside reverse folds.

3. Cut front layers and valley fold to open.

4. Turn over.

5. Pleat folds.

6. Valley fold.

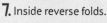

7. Inside reverse folds.

8. Inside reverse folds.

9. Mountain fold in half.

10. Inside reverse fold.

11. Valley fold both sides.

12. Crimp fold.

13. Crimp fold.

14. Crimp fold.

15. Valley fold.

16. Turn over.

17. Valley fold.

18. Completed PART 2.

ASSEMBLY

1. Join parts together as shown and apply glue to hold.

2. Completed ALIEN.

WEREWOLF

You only see him late at night. He runs around like crazy and he's always thrashing about. This guy likes to party!

PART 1

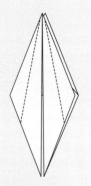

1. Start with Base Fold 3. Valley folds.

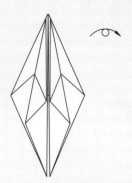

2. Turn over.

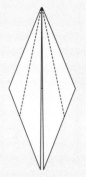

3. Valley folds.

4. Cut top layer as shown.

5. Valley fold to open out.

6. Cut the top flap.

7. Valley folds.

8. Valley folds.

9. Valley fold.

10. Turn over.

11. Pleat fold.

12. Valley fold in half.

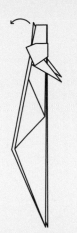

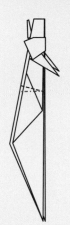

13. Pull "mouth" open and squash into position.

14. Cut tip as shown.

15. Crimp fold.

16. Rotate.

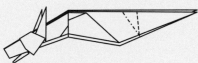
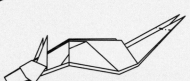
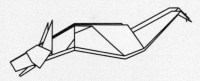

17. Crimp fold both sides.

18. Inside reverse fold both sides.

19. Outside reverse fold both sides.

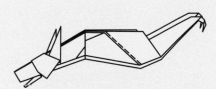

20. Valley fold top layer.

21. Turn over.

22. Valley fold top layer.

23. Completed PART 1.

PART 2

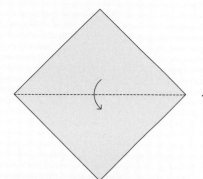

1. Valley fold square
   (same size as PART I)
   in half.

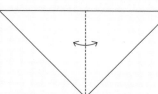

2. Valley fold and unfold.

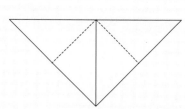

3. Valley folds.

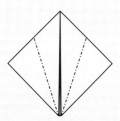

4. Inside reverse folds.

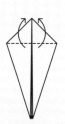

5. Valley folds.

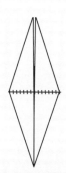

6. Cut top layers
   as shown.

7. Valley folds.

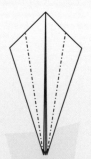

8. Inside reverse folds.

9. Valley folds.

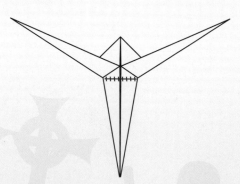

10. Cut front layers only.

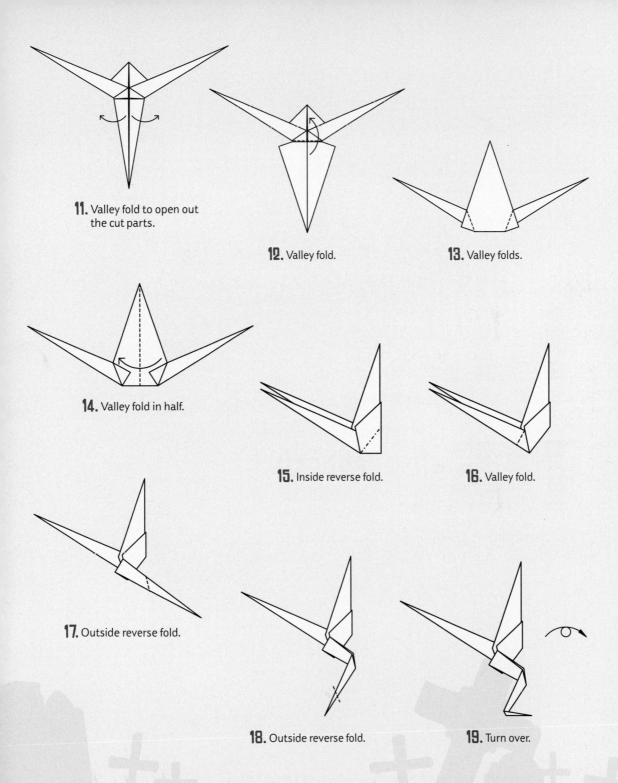

11. Valley fold to open out the cut parts.

12. Valley fold.

13. Valley folds.

14. Valley fold in half.

15. Inside reverse fold.

16. Valley fold.

17. Outside reverse fold.

18. Outside reverse fold.

19. Turn over.

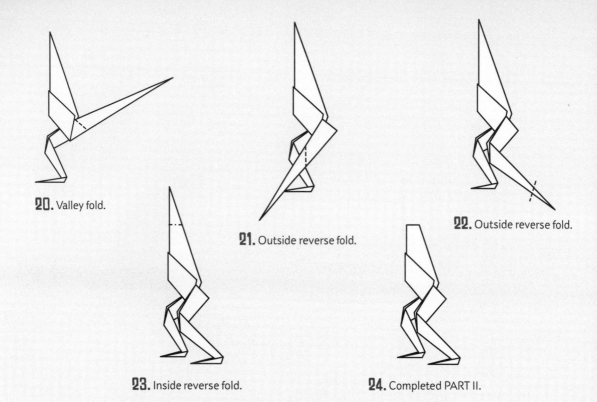

20. Valley fold.

21. Outside reverse fold.

22. Outside reverse fold.

23. Inside reverse fold.

24. Completed PART II.

ASSEMBLY

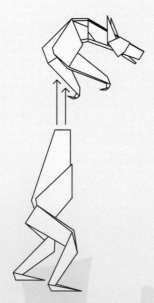

1. Join both parts together as shown and apply glue to hold.

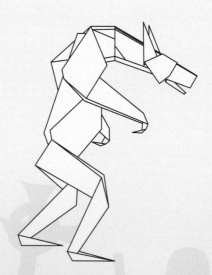

2. Completed WEREWOLF.

INDEX

A
Alien, *112–116*

B
Base folds, 12–16
    about: legend explaining
        symbols, 8
    base fold 1, 12
    base fold 2, 13
    base fold 3, 14
    base fold 4, 15
    base fold 5, 16
    sink fold, 13
Black Lagoon, creature from,
    81–87

C
Creature from the Black
    Lagoon, *81–87*

D
Demon, *88–95*
Dracula, *103–111*
Dragon, three-headed,
    96–102

F
Folds
    about: legend explaining
        symbols, 8
    base fold 1, 12
    base fold 2, 13
    base fold 3, 14
    base fold 4, 15
    base fold 5, 16
    inside crimp fold, 11
    inside reverse fold, 9
    kite fold, 8
    mountain fold, 8
    outside crimp fold, 11
    outside reverse fold, 9
    pleat fold, 10
    pleat fold reversed, 10
    sink fold, 13
    squash fold 1, 10
    squash fold 2, 11
    valley fold, 8
Frankenstein's Monster,
    74–80

G
Glue tips, 7

H
Headless Horseman, *17–29*

I
Inside crimp fold, 11
Inside reverse fold, 9

K
Kite fold, 8

L
Legend, for fold diagrams, 8

M
Mountain fold, 8
Mummy, *30–37*

O
Outside crimp fold, 11
Outside reverse fold, 9

P
Paper tips, 7
Pleat fold, 10
Pleat fold reversed, 10
Projects
    Alien, *112–116*
    Creature from the Black
        Lagoon, *81–87*
    Demon, *88–95*
    Dracula, *103–111*
    Frankenstein's Monster,
        74–80
    Headless Horseman, *17–29*
    Mummy, *30–37*
    Scarecrow, *38–49*
    Three-Headed Dragon,
        96–102
    Werewolf, *117–122*
    Witch, *50–57*
    Wolf Man, *58–65*
    Zombie, *66–73*

S
Scarecrow, *38–49*
Sink fold, 13
Squash fold 1, 10
Squash fold 2, 11
Symbols, legend explaining, 8

T
Technique tips, 7
Three-Headed Dragon,
    96–102

V
Valley fold, 8

W
Werewolf, *117–122*
Witch, *50–57*
Wolf Man, *58–65*

Z
Zombie, *66–73*